THIS BOOK BELONGS TO

_____

DATE STARTED

_____

The world is full of magical things patiently
waiting for our senses to get sharper.

W.B. YEATS, poet (1865–1934)

PROLOGUE

The modern-day nature explorer is not one who takes birds' eggs or catches butterflies. He or she is merely a guardian of the countryside – an adventurer who is thrilled at the sight of a soaring bird, who lies on the grass watching the stars and who gleefully crunches through freshly fallen snow. He or she is someone who enjoys sensing the infinite variety of the natural world and who gathers objects sensitively and only when doing so won't harm the environment. For nature explorers such as this, the pages of this book are waiting to be completed.

WITH THANKS TO

David Burnie – Natural-history consultant
Sunita Gahir – Production adviser
Penny Phillips – Proofreader
Steve Dilworth – For skulls & exciting parcels
The Bounce Team – For boundless sales enthusiasm
Michael Guiry – For seaweed expertise & other advice

The elusive lacewing

First published in 2016 by Fine Feather Press Limited
The Coach House, Elstead Road, Farnham, Surrey GU10 1JE
Copyright © 2016 Fine Feather Press Limited

10 9 8 7 6 5 4 3 2 1

A CIP catalogue record is available from the British Library
ISBN: 978-1-9084-8926-5
Printed and bound in Shenzhen, China, by WKT

www.finefeatherpress.com

WHAT LIES INSIDE

ABOUT THIS BOOK

*No one will protect what they don't care about and no one
will care about what they have never experienced.*
Sir David Attenborough, naturalist (born 1926)

This book comes with a promise: once you start looking closely at the natural world, you will never be bored again. Animals, plants, rocks, the weather – they will all catch your eye in ways you cannot begin to imagine. Yet this book is only the beginning: a leaping-off point to a world that will never tire of revealing new wonders. We hope you enjoy the journey.

BEING OUTSIDE

You do not need much for a nature walk, but you might find a few things useful, such as a backpack, collecting bags, binoculars, sketch book and a camera or phone with which to take pictures. Patience is the key to nature-watching, so walk slowly and use all your senses. Every day is different and if you can't find what you want or don't seem to see much, keep looking. Tomorrow will definitely not be the same as today.

TAKING NATURE PHOTOGRAPHS

Taking photographs is a wonderful way to record your nature experiences without disturbing animals or their habitats. Everyone can take a photograph, but not everyone can take a good one. Here are a few useful tips: get in close to your subject; decide what part of it you want to focus on; keep very still; experiment with angles; and take lots of shots – you can delete the ones you don't want later.

WHAT TO DO WHEN YOU GET HOME

One of the best moments is arriving back after a trip out and trying to work out what you have seen or collected. Guide books and the internet are extremely helpful but it can be a dark art, so don't expect to identify everything immediately. Stick what you can in this book, and for larger items use a shelf or an area at home to display your findings. Remember to date and label everything possible – what it is and when and where it was found. Above all, share your discoveries with friends – you'll be amazed at what people will give in return.

THE NATURE EXPLORER'S CODE

*The frog does not drink up the
pond in which it lives.*
INDIAN PROVERB

BASIC SAFETY

This scrapbook is about experiencing nature. It is a book of dos, not don'ts. However, staying safe should always be your first concern. Some things are poisonous, some places are unsafe, some weather is dangerous to go out in. Always tell an adult where you are and what you are doing.

COLLECTING SPECIMENS

Whether you are gathering flowers, fungi or the remains and traces of animals, check that they are things that you are allowed to take. Your local countryside laws are available online and will list what these are. Don't take any more of anything than you need, and make sure you leave areas that you visit as you found them.

CARING FOR THE COUNTRYSIDE

Britain has an incredible network of public footpaths and nature reserves. Keep to waymarked routes, shut gates behind you and ask permission to access private land. Leaving litter or any other signs of your visit risks damaging the wildlife that lives there and is unsightly.

MAKING UNUSUAL DISCOVERIES

If you make an exciting find, make sure you tell a local nature organisation. However, it is as well to remember that not everyone cares for the planet as you do, so keep secret the location of anything that might get distressed, damaged or stolen if its whereabouts were publicly known.

Mammal tracks & signs

Colours in nature

EARTH

THERE ARE NO PASSENGERS ON
SPACESHIP EARTH. WE ARE ALL CREW.

Marshall McLuhan, philosopher (1911–1980)

The Earth is a mere dot in space but a varied and vast playground for us humans. On the pages that follow, you will find a guide to some of the things you can look out for on your journeys outside. From the simplest pebble to the most ancient fossil, there is a huge world that awaits you. Not everything can be collected, yet there are no limits to the adventures you can have discovering the things that lie beneath your feet.

Tree leaves

Seeds

Minerals & fossils

Flowers

Grasses

Nature's patterns

Skulls

Rocks

Capturing time

MY EARTH COLLECTION

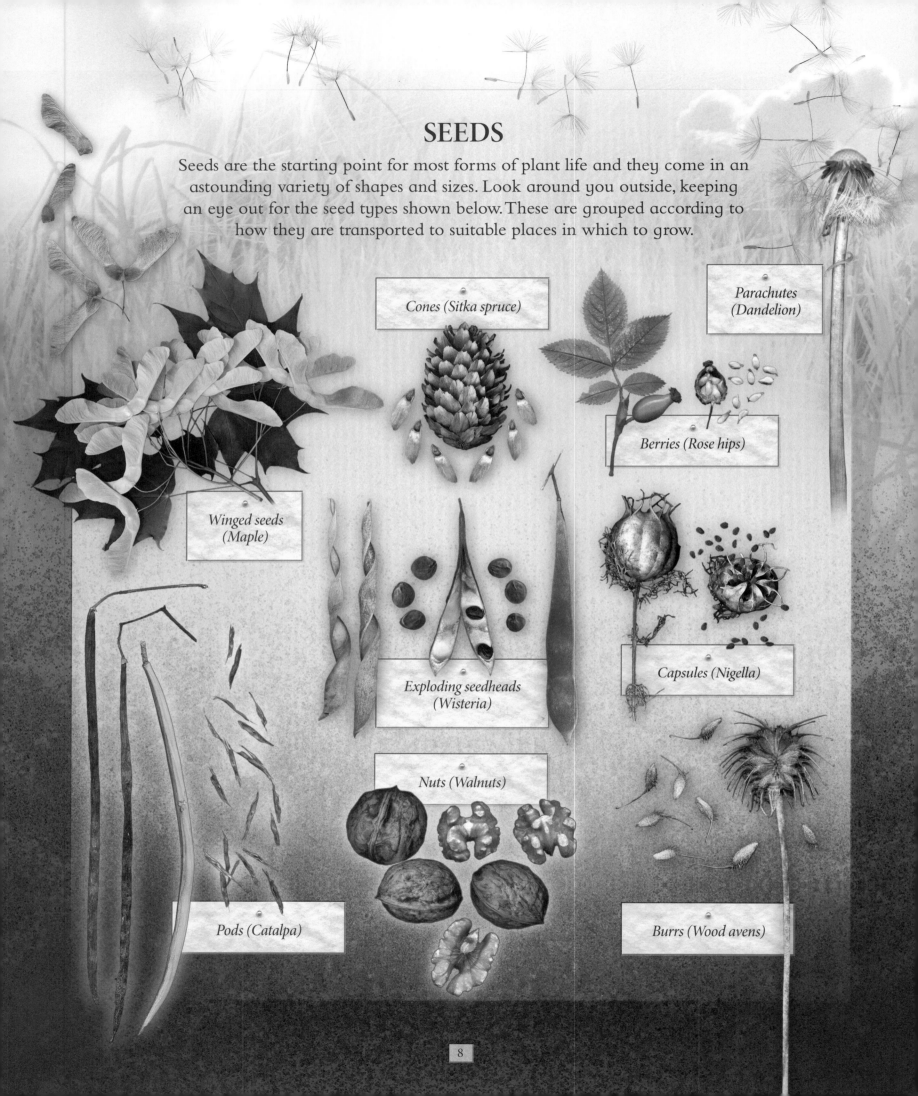

SEEDS

Seeds are the starting point for most forms of plant life and they come in an astounding variety of shapes and sizes. Look around you outside, keeping an eye out for the seed types shown below. These are grouped according to how they are transported to suitable places in which to grow.

Cones (Sitka spruce)

Parachutes (Dandelion)

Berries (Rose hips)

Winged seeds (Maple)

Exploding seedheads (Wisteria)

Capsules (Nigella)

Nuts (Walnuts)

Pods (Catalpa)

Burrs (Wood avens)

HOW TO COLLECT SEEDS

Seeds can be fun to collect and they have the added bonus of being completely free. Here are some tips on how to gather and store different seed types. You can then use them to create new plants the next growing season, or to make interesting pictures.

Lotus seedpods

Poppy seeds

PODS, CONES AND CAPSULES

Pick seedheads when they are mature but before they open, then lay them out to dry in a warm place. They may open automatically or you can split them to release the seeds inside. Place cones in a warm spot on a sheet of paper. The seeds inside should fall out as the cone opens.

Beech mast

FRUITS, NUTS AND BERRIES

Split open firm fruit such as apples and pears to pick out the seeds inside. Gather ripe nuts from trees or pick up windfalls from the ground. Push berries through a sieve, then rinse away the pulp and leave the seeds out to dry. Remember that you will need to gather these before the birds do!

Cranberries

EXPLODING SEED HEADS

Exploding seedheads are pretty exciting to see opening. If you want to collect the seeds from these plants, pick the heads just before they ripen and place them in a bag. Check them every few days and give them a good shake to encourage them to open.

Wild strawberries

Rape seeds

HOW TO STORE SEEDS

Clean away any dirt from your seeds and place them in labelled paper packets in an airtight container, then store them in a cool place until required. Most seeds can be kept like this for several years.

Young coconut

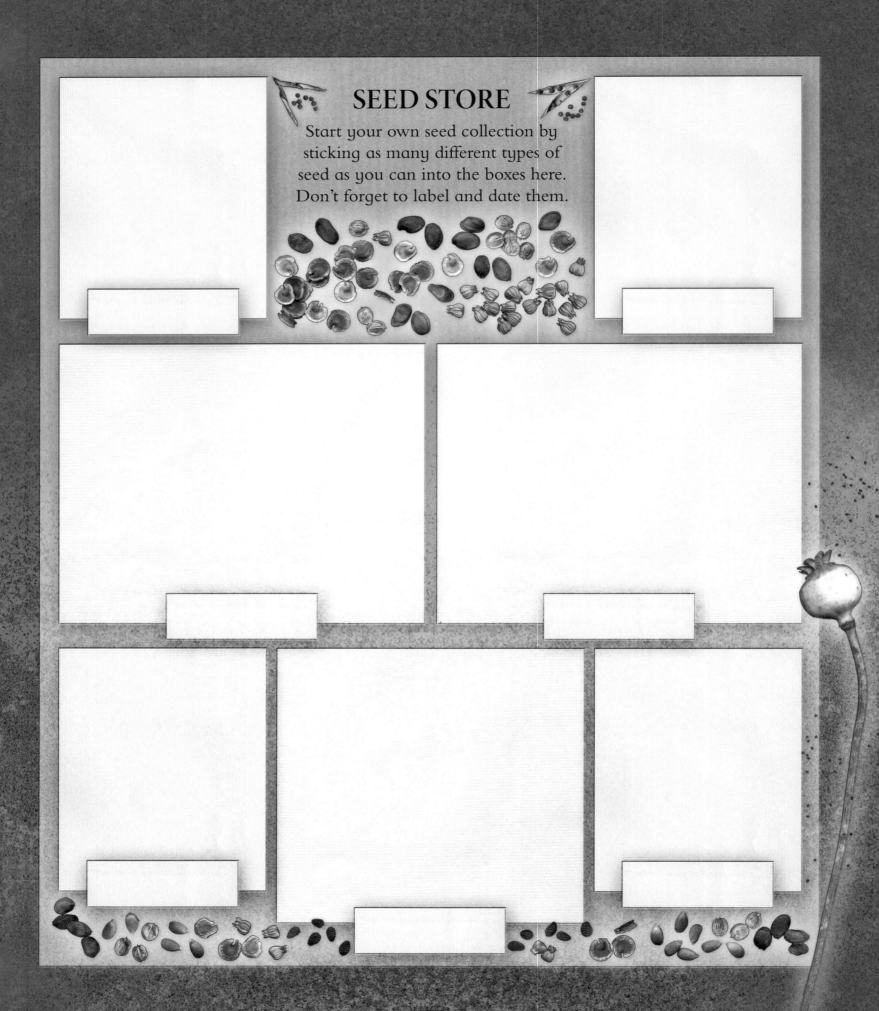

SEED STORE

Start your own seed collection by
sticking as many different types of
seed as you can into the boxes here.
Don't forget to label and date them.

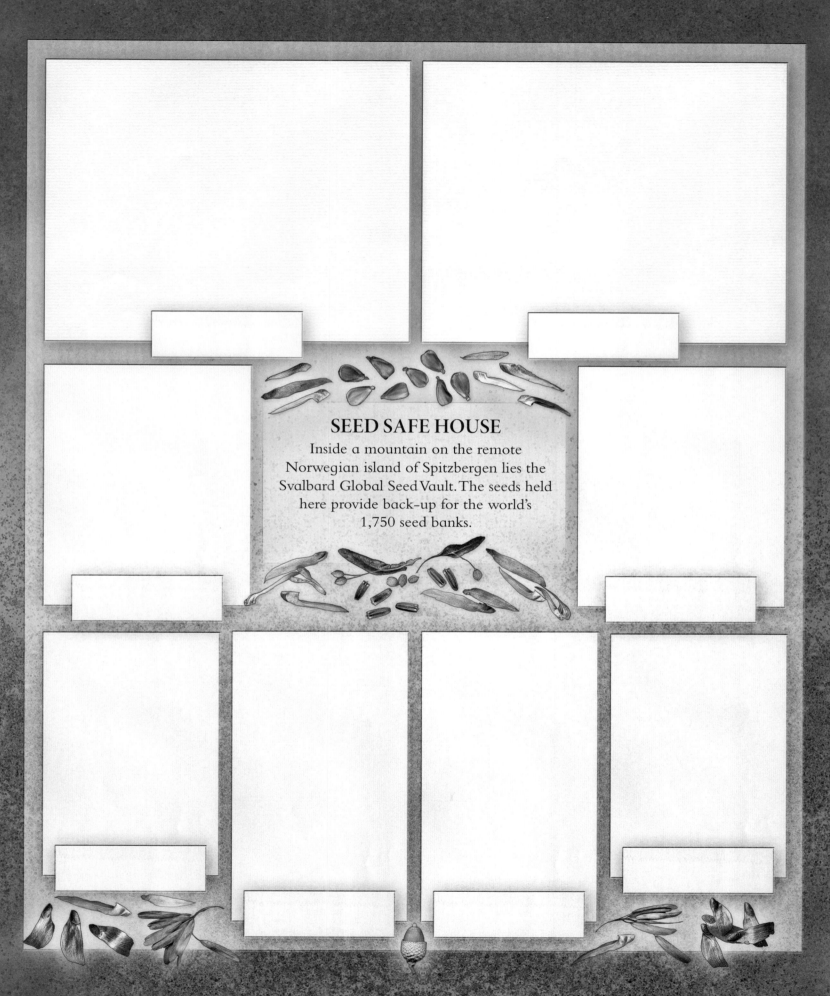

SEED SAFE HOUSE

Inside a mountain on the remote Norwegian island of Spitzbergen lies the Svalbard Global Seed Vault. The seeds held here provide back-up for the world's 1,750 seed banks.

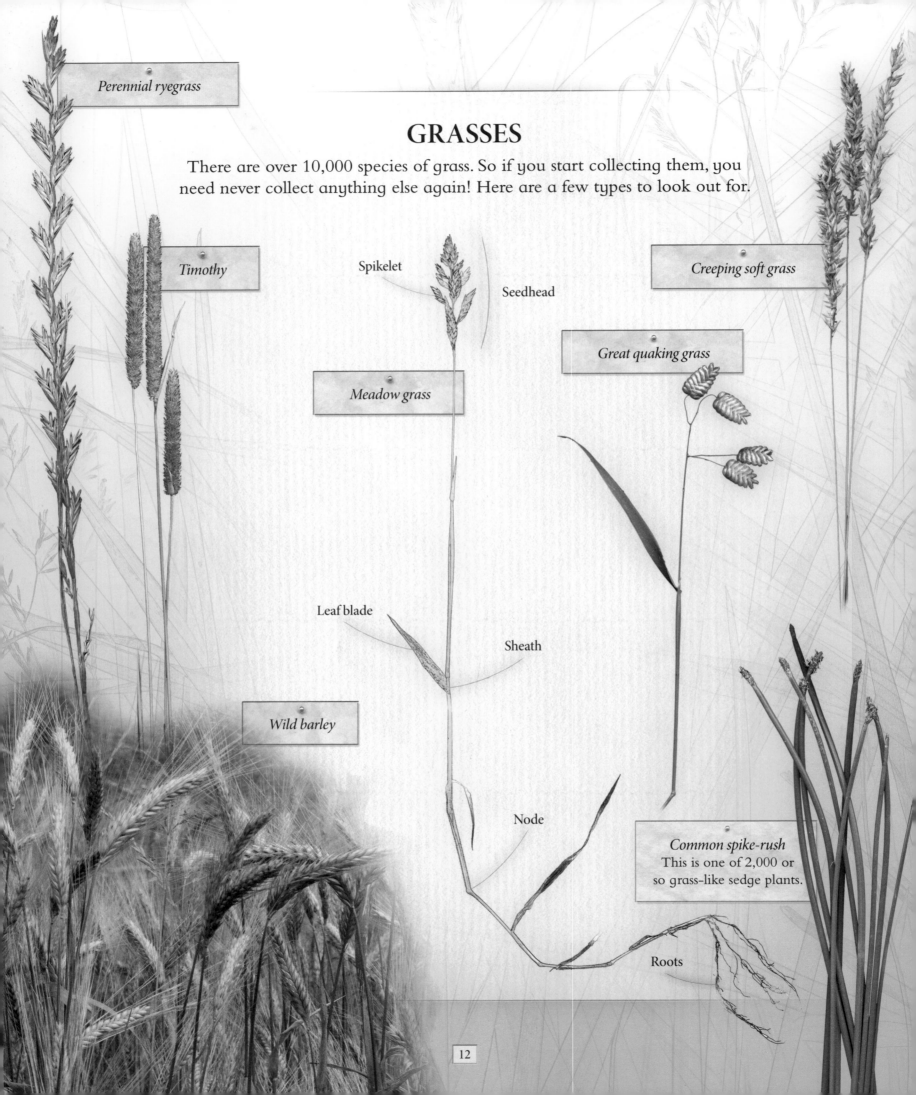

GRASSES

There are over 10,000 species of grass. So if you start collecting them, you need never collect anything else again! Here are a few types to look out for.

Perennial ryegrass

Timothy

Spikelet

Seedhead

Creeping soft grass

Great quaking grass

Meadow grass

Leaf blade

Sheath

Wild barley

Node

Common spike-rush
This is one of 2,000 or so grass-like sedge plants.

Roots

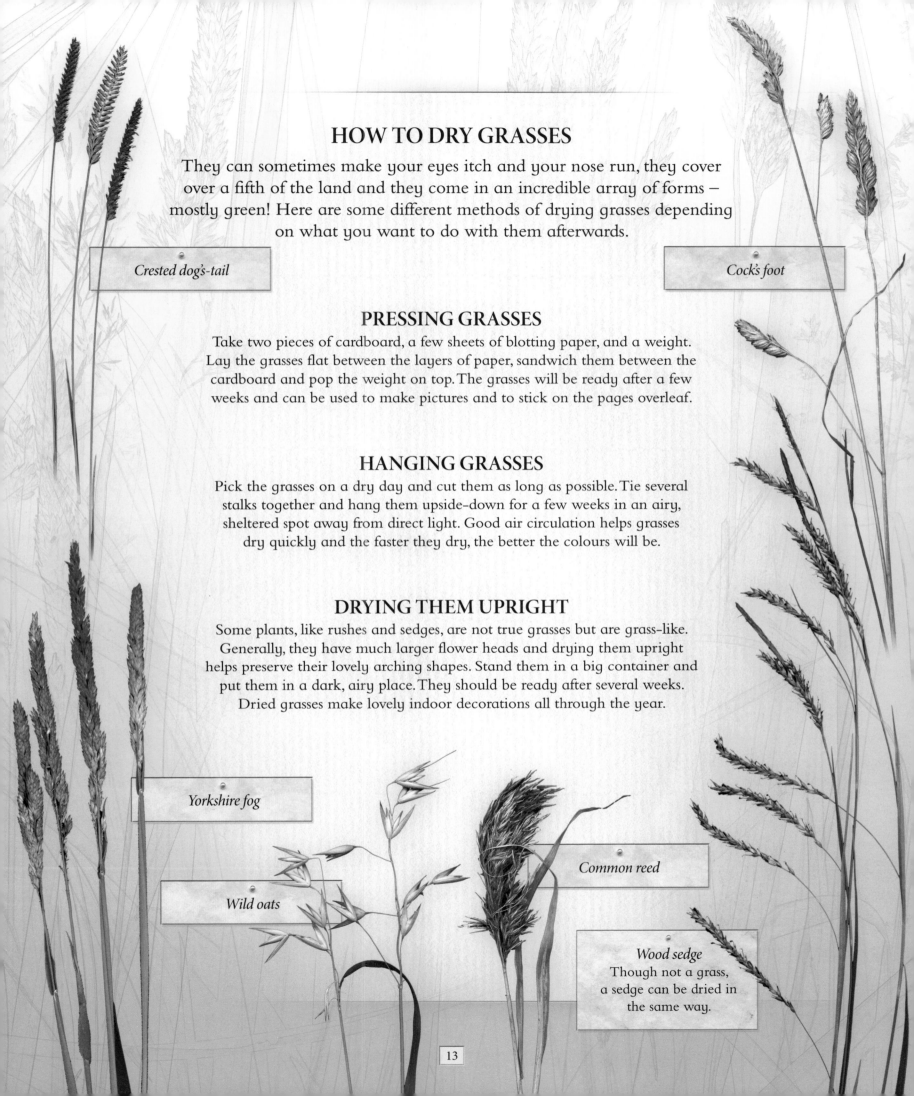

HOW TO DRY GRASSES

They can sometimes make your eyes itch and your nose run, they cover over a fifth of the land and they come in an incredible array of forms – mostly green! Here are some different methods of drying grasses depending on what you want to do with them afterwards.

Crested dog's-tail

Cock's foot

PRESSING GRASSES

Take two pieces of cardboard, a few sheets of blotting paper, and a weight. Lay the grasses flat between the layers of paper, sandwich them between the cardboard and pop the weight on top. The grasses will be ready after a few weeks and can be used to make pictures and to stick on the pages overleaf.

HANGING GRASSES

Pick the grasses on a dry day and cut them as long as possible. Tie several stalks together and hang them upside-down for a few weeks in an airy, sheltered spot away from direct light. Good air circulation helps grasses dry quickly and the faster they dry, the better the colours will be.

DRYING THEM UPRIGHT

Some plants, like rushes and sedges, are not true grasses but are grass-like. Generally, they have much larger flower heads and drying them upright helps preserve their lovely arching shapes. Stand them in a big container and put them in a dark, airy place. They should be ready after several weeks. Dried grasses make lovely indoor decorations all through the year.

Yorkshire fog

Wild oats

Common reed

Wood sedge
Though not a grass, a sedge can be dried in the same way.

Forget-me-nots

FLOWERS

Pressing flowers means that you can enjoy them for a long time. Check local countryside laws before picking wild flowers and preferably take ones from your own garden if you have one. Don't forget that so-called weeds are also flowers – just in the "wrong" place – and look lovely when pressed.

Cranesbills

Hydrangeas

Brambles

Hellebores

Pansies

Buttercups

CHOOSING THE BEST FLOWERS

Flowers with thin petals arranged in a single circle like most of the ones shown here generally press better than thicker ones. Other flowers you could try are borage, larkspur, verbenas, poppies, wild carrot, cornflowers, love-in-a-mist and violas. Alternatively, just keep experimenting. Leaves also work well such as the younger, fresher leaves of ferns, ivy, maple and ginkgo.

Ferns

Clover leaves

HOW TO PRESS FLOWERS

The best time to pick flowers and leaves for pressing is when they are at their driest, after the dew has evaporated in the morning. Choose the youngest, freshest, most colourful flowers that are free from damage and cut each stem as close to the flower head as possible.

CREATING A PRESS

You can buy a press but it is just as easy to place your flowers face-down between two sheets of blotting paper, making sure there is space between each flower. Place a heavy weight on top to create your press.

Cosmos

Pressed flowers

Foxglove florets

USING YOUR PRESSED FLOWERS

Leave the flowers for at least two or three weeks, then carefully open up your press. If you are happy that they are ready, gently remove them. Arrange them further using glue and tweezers to create an array of cards, bookmarks, pictures to frame, candle or egg decorations. Alternatively, you can use the following pages for storing or displaying your flowers.

17

FLOWER DISPLAY

SKULLS

It is exciting, if slightly ghoulish, to come across animal carcasses or bones.
However, they do liven up any natural-history collection. It is always a
good idea to make sure you have cleaned any specimens thoroughly
before you display them.

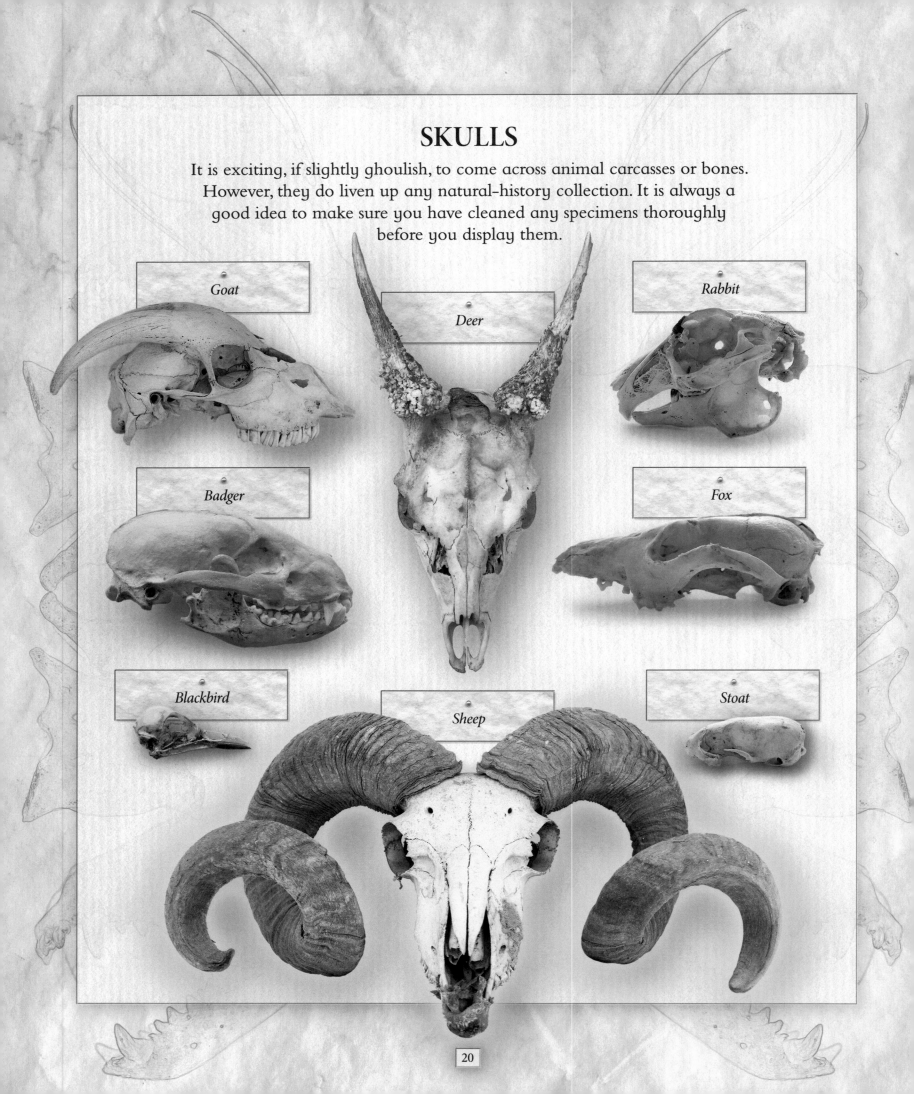

Goat

Deer

Rabbit

Badger

Fox

Blackbird

Sheep

Stoat

Ribs

HOW TO CLEAN ANIMAL BONES

Some of the tips below are not for the faint-hearted but can yield surprisingly good results. Maggots may not be appealing but they are the life-blood of natural decomposition and they are much better at getting the flesh off animals than we are!

Otter

Razorbill

DEALING WITH AN ANIMAL CARCASS

Dead animals left on the ground rot down well, although you will need to find a way to prevent other animals from carrying them away. Alternatively, try burying the remains (remembering the location is key) and then digging them up about three months later. Nature should have done much of the cleaning work for you.

Greylag goose

Goldfinch

Vertebrae

CLEANING UP ANIMAL BONES

If the bones you find have any soft tissue left on them, biological washing powder is the best way to get rid of it. Mix some in a bucket of hot water and leave the bones to soak for a few days. Rinse the bones really well and then dry them. Repeat if necessary before adding the bones to your collection.

Mole

Mouse

TREATING ANTLERS

If the antlers still have velvet on them, make sure you strip it off before soaking them. Then completely submerge them in warm water with biological washing powder for a day or so. Take them out and leave them to dry in the light. You could also try boiling them in bleach to both harden and clean them.

Red deer antler

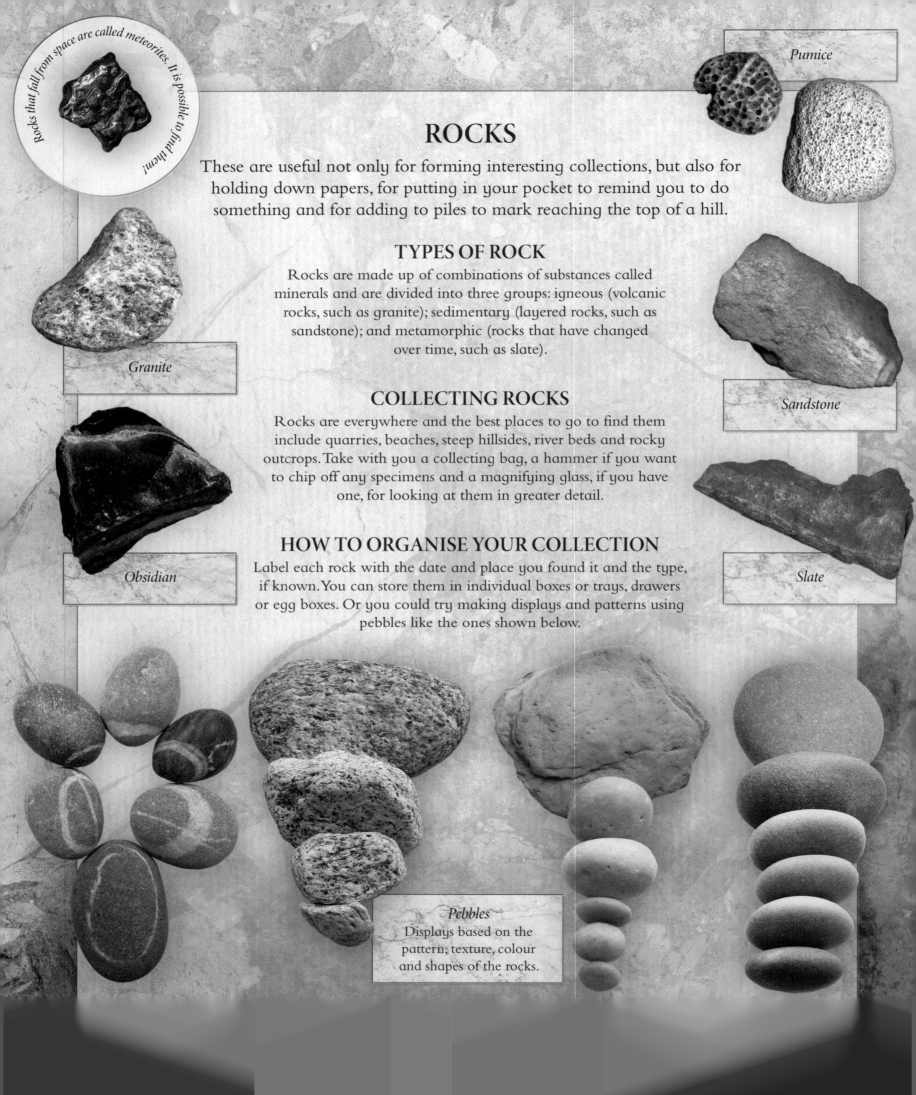

Rocks that fall from space are called meteorites. It is possible to find them!

Pumice

ROCKS

These are useful not only for forming interesting collections, but also for holding down papers, for putting in your pocket to remind you to do something and for adding to piles to mark reaching the top of a hill.

TYPES OF ROCK

Rocks are made up of combinations of substances called minerals and are divided into three groups: igneous (volcanic rocks, such as granite); sedimentary (layered rocks, such as sandstone); and metamorphic (rocks that have changed over time, such as slate).

Granite

Sandstone

COLLECTING ROCKS

Rocks are everywhere and the best places to go to find them include quarries, beaches, steep hillsides, river beds and rocky outcrops. Take with you a collecting bag, a hammer if you want to chip off any specimens and a magnifying glass, if you have one, for looking at them in greater detail.

Obsidian

Slate

HOW TO ORGANISE YOUR COLLECTION

Label each rock with the date and place you found it and the type, if known. You can store them in individual boxes or trays, drawers or egg boxes. Or you could try making displays and patterns using pebbles like the ones shown below.

Pebbles
Displays based on the pattern, texture, colour and shapes of the rocks.

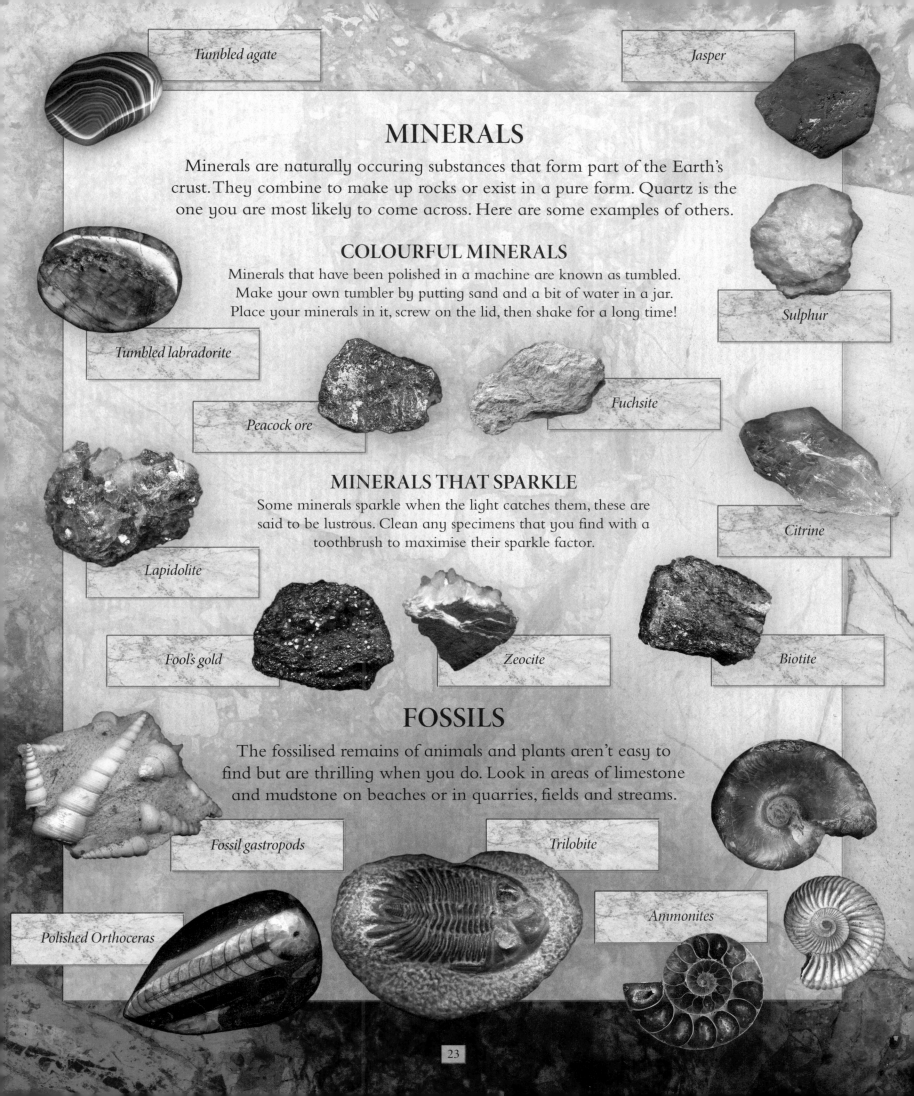

Tumbled agate

Jasper

MINERALS

Minerals are naturally occuring substances that form part of the Earth's crust. They combine to make up rocks or exist in a pure form. Quartz is the one you are most likely to come across. Here are some examples of others.

COLOURFUL MINERALS

Minerals that have been polished in a machine are known as tumbled. Make your own tumbler by putting sand and a bit of water in a jar. Place your minerals in it, screw on the lid, then shake for a long time!

Sulphur

Tumbled labradorite

Fuchsite

Peacock ore

Citrine

MINERALS THAT SPARKLE

Some minerals sparkle when the light catches them, these are said to be lustrous. Clean any specimens that you find with a toothbrush to maximise their sparkle factor.

Lapidolite

Biotite

Fool's gold

Zeocite

FOSSILS

The fossilised remains of animals and plants aren't easy to find but are thrilling when you do. Look in areas of limestone and mudstone on beaches or in quarries, fields and streams.

Fossil gastropods

Trilobite

Ammonites

Polished Orthoceras

TREE LEAVES

Leaves make food for plants. They come in many different shapes, colours and sizes and each is suited to the environment it grows in. Here are some of the main features to look out for when you are collecting leaves.

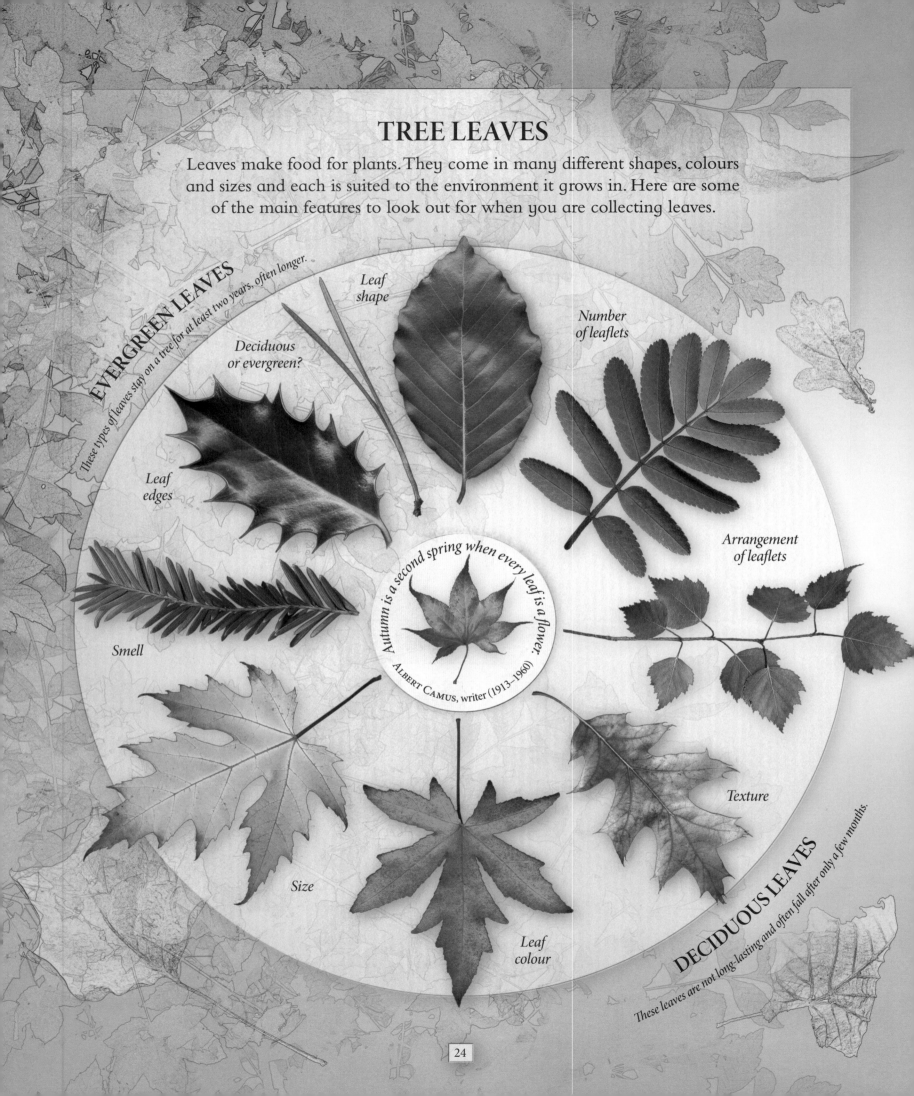

EVERGREEN LEAVES
These types of leaves stay on a tree for at least two years, often longer.

Deciduous or evergreen?

Leaf shape

Number of leaflets

Leaf edges

Arrangement of leaflets

Smell

Autumn is a second spring when every leaf is a flower.
ALBERT CAMUS, writer (1913–1960)

Size

Leaf colour

Texture

DECIDUOUS LEAVES
These leaves are not long-lasting and often fall after only a few months.

LEAF ACTIVITIES

Tree leaves are colourful, fun and free. Possible ideas for things to do with them are given below, or you can simply enjoy kicking your feet through piles of them on crisp autumn and winter days.

Ginkgo

Aspen

Cotinus

Maple

Poplar

PRESSING LEAVES

Hawthorn

Pressing leaves is very similar to pressing flowers. Collect some interesting leaves and put them between two pieces of blotting paper. Place a heavy weight on top and leave them for a couple of weeks. You can use the pressed leaves to make pictures, bookmarks or other decorations.

Cherry

LEAF RUBBING

To get an idea of how the veins of a leaf are arranged, try doing a leaf rubbing. Turn a leaf upside-down and place a piece of paper over the top of it. Rub the paper with a crayon and see the vein pattern appear. Label your pattern with the type of leaf and then find some different ones to do.

SKELETON LEAVES

Willow

This fairly simple trick will create some fascinating skeleton leaves. Put 600 ml (1 pt) of water into a saucepan and add 100 g (4 oz) of washing powder. Boil the leaves for 20 minutes, then rinse and tease away the pulp with a toothbrush to leave a skeleton shape.

Sycamore skeleton

Eucalyptus

Sweet chestnut

Avocado

LEAF LIBRARY

EVERGREEN LEAVES

DECIDUOUS LEAVES

Overlapping patterns

Waves

Stripes

Branches

Spheres

To understand is to perceive patterns.

Sɪʀ Isᴀɪᴀʜ Bᴇʀʟɪɴ, philosopher (1909–1997)

NATURE'S PATTERNS

Once you start looking for patterns in the natural world, it's difficult to stop. Animal patterns are usually there for a good reason – often to prevent them from being seen and eaten or to impress a mate. Plants also evolve patterns over time to make them more appealing to the insects that pollinate them.

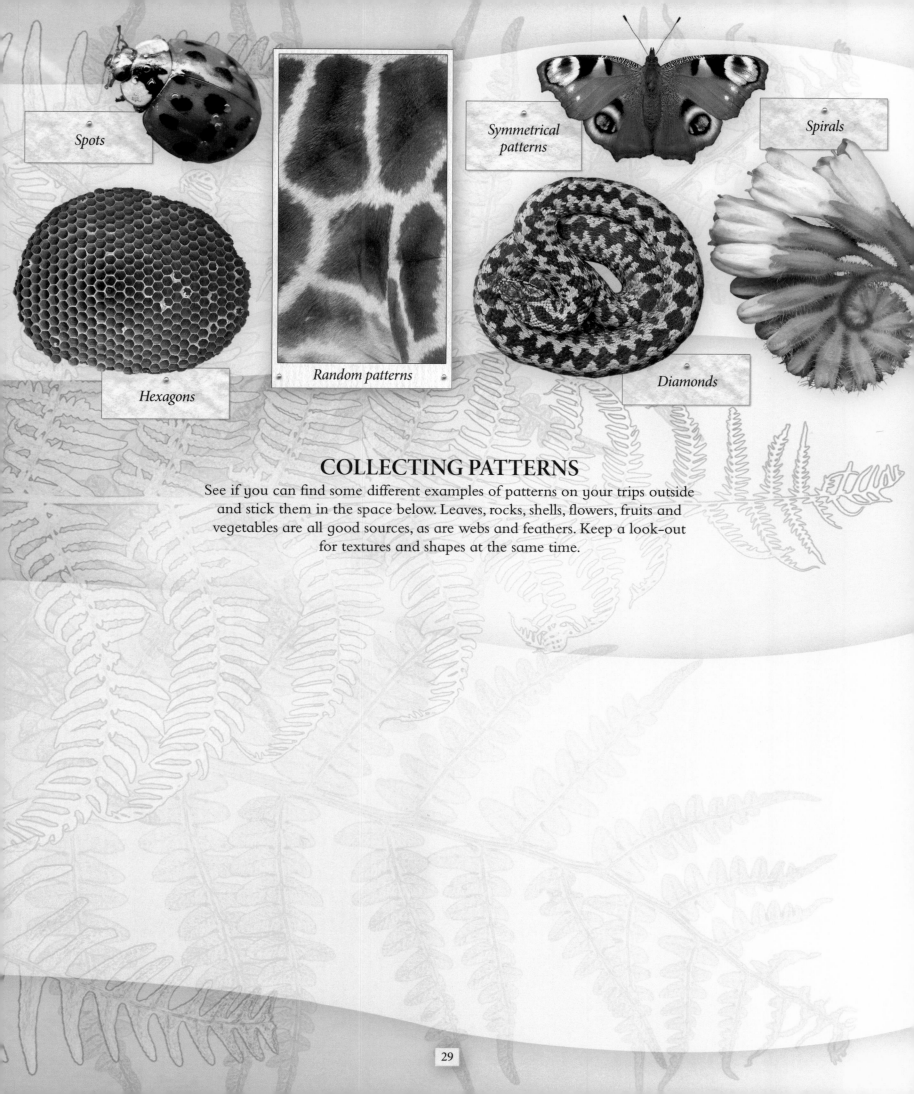

Spots

Symmetrical patterns

Spirals

Hexagons

Random patterns

Diamonds

COLLECTING PATTERNS

See if you can find some different examples of patterns on your trips outside
and stick them in the space below. Leaves, rocks, shells, flowers, fruits and
vegetables are all good sources, as are webs and feathers. Keep a look-out
for textures and shapes at the same time.

COLOURS IN NATURE

If you turn over the page, you will find a space to create your own colour collection based on the objects you find outside. This could include items such as feathers, leaves, dead insects and shells. For more three-dimensional objects, why not take pictures of them to stick in instead? You could also create a colour chart like the one shown here to compare a range of colours. Alternatively, you could concentrate on one single colour – green might be a particularly rewarding one to choose.

Crimson raspberry

Red tomato

Orange flames

Golden maple leaf

Brown cow

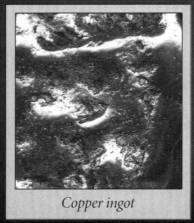
Copper ingot

Ochre rock

Yellow dandelion

Maroon petals

SPLITTING WHITE LIGHT

It was Sir Isaac Newton (1643–1727) – an English physicist, alchemist and mathematician – who discovered that white light is made up of seven colours: red, orange, yellow, green, blue, indigo and violet. This is most easily seen when a rainbow appears. You could make a rainbow by placing a mirror inside a glass in a darkened room and shining a torch through the glass on to the mirror.

Beige grass seeds

Olive green crab

Aquamarine stream

Deep blue sea

Light blue sky

Lime green moss

WHAT DO YOU SEE?

Try sitting down with an animal or flower guide book and browse through the names. Some of them can be quite misleading from a colour perspective. Did the person who named the red squirrel really see the same red that you see? It is difficult to know whether people observe colours differently unless they are obviously colour blind.

Vision is the art of seeing what is invisible to everyone else.
<small>JONATHAN SWIFT, writer (1667–1745)</small>

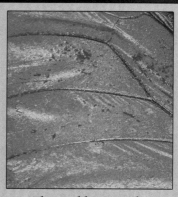
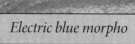
Electric blue morpho

Emerald green boa

Pink flamingo

Mauve mushroom

Purple crocuses

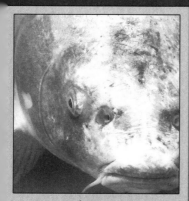
Silver carp

White sheep

Grey cygnet

Black cat

RAINBOW COLLECTION

MAMMAL TRACKS & SIGNS

Every walk outside can easily be turned into a game of detection. The best place to start is near your home, where you can get to know the land well. Mammals, like all animals, leave clues wherever they go, some of which are more obvious than others. Here are a few signs to keep an eye out for.

DROPPINGS

These are an easy way to tell what animals have been in the area. Don't handle them, just make a note of their shape, colour, texture and location, then look them up on your return. Plant-eater droppings are usually round and fibrous, whereas meat-eater ones tend to be longer and significantly smellier.

Rabbit droppings

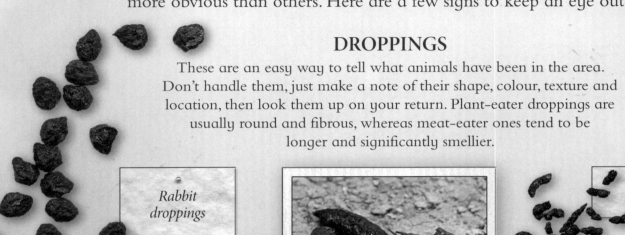

Fox scat

Bat guano

HOMES

Winter is the best time to see mammal homes, when the vegetation has died back. Check whether there is freshly-dug earth or food remains outside animal holes or any tracks to help you identify the occupants.

Otter holt

Squirrel drey

Badger sett

TRACKS

Mammal tracks show up best in snow, mud or wet sand. You can make a cast of them using plaster of Paris or keep notes and drawings in a notebook. Check the number of toes, signs of claw marks and whether the prints are together or alternating. This tells you whether an animal walks or hops.

Dog tracks

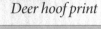
Deer hoof print

FOOD REMAINS

Look out for part-eaten nuts, pine cones, fruit, fungi and seeds in the autumn and raided eggshells and nibbled plant shoots in the spring and summer. Gather the food remains and make a collection of them at home.

Hazelnut shells

Raided egg

Cone stalks

OTHER SIGNS

Animal paths criss-cross the land; it may be easier to see them when the grass is long in the spring and summer. Mole hills are easy to spot; look out also for marks on trees where deer rub their antlers and check fences and branches for signs of fur or wool.

Sheep wool

Mole hills

Antler rubbings

CAPTURING TIME

Time-lapse photography is where you take a sequence of photos to either seemingly slow down or speed up a sequence of events. In nature, this allows you to re-live the actual passing of time as well as to study life processes that you otherwise wouldn't be able to see. It is also incredibly easy to do.

A donkey rolling (15 seconds)

CHOOSING YOUR SUBJECT

Anything that grows, decays or moves, such as trees, flowers, animals and the weather, would be excellent to photograph. First, work out how long you want to spend. Photographing a decaying flower takes a lot longer than snapping a moving animal. Here are some suggestions and on page 58 there is also a time-lapse light sequence.

A buttercup turning to seed (several days)

A deciduous tree through the seasons (1 year)

WHAT YOU NEED

Patience is required and some sort of device for taking images. Once you have decided on your subject, compose your scene and ensure your camera is set in the same place for each shot. A professional would use a tripod, but a steady surface works just as well.

Snow falling in a garden (7 hours)

CAPTURING TIME INSIDE

Flowers, fruit, small animals and leaves are all good subjects to use for inside shots. Arrange your scene in a place where it won't get disturbed and try some sample pictures with different backgrounds to see which ones look best. Keep your comera still and take far more shots than you need, then choose the best ones.

A leaf decaying (3 days)

TAKING SEQUENCES OUTSIDE

You cannot plan for many outdoor sequences as they often involve spontaneous events such as birds in flight or sudden weather sequences, so be prepared for anything at any time. If you have a large number of photos, you could try making a flick book.

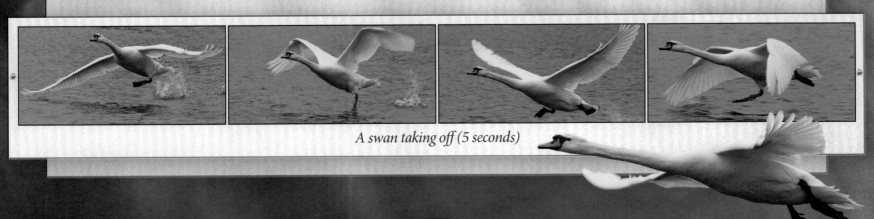

A swan taking off (5 seconds)

Clouds

Spores

Moths

AIR

THE BEST REMEDY FOR THOSE WHO ARE AFRAID, LONELY, OR UNHAPPY IS TO GO OUTSIDE.
ANNE FRANK, writer (1929–1945)

If the day isn't going your way or something's niggling you, step outside and take a deep breath. Few things restore the spirit as much as fresh air, whatever the season or the time of day. In the pages that follow, you can take a trip through the sky looking at clouds, birds and insects, or search for traces of the places aerial creatures have been in the form of regurgitated pellets and strange exoskeletons called exuviae.

Feathers

Butterflies

Exuviae

From dawn to dusk

Other insects

Owl pellets

MY AIR COLLECTION

Cirrus

Cirrostratus

Altostratus

Altocumulus

Cumulonimbus

CLOUDS

Cloud names are based on how high clouds are and what they look like. Cumulus clouds are tall and heaped with curvy tops. Stratus clouds are long, thin and layered. Cirrus clouds are wispy and curled, and nimbus clouds bring rain. High clouds have names starting with "cirro" and mid-layer clouds with "alto". Create your own cloud gallery on the page opposite.

Cumulus

Nimbostratus

CLOUD QUEST

FEATHERS

Birds moult about once a year, usually at the end of the breeding season.
This is when you are likely to find some pretty shabby-looking birds.
Moulting helps them to replace worn or damaged feathers and this is
a good time to find feathers lying on the ground.

Green woodpecker

Mallard

Chaffinch

Goldfinch

Hoopoe

Owl

Ring-necked parakeet

Pheasant

Jay

Canary

Magpie

Crow

Great spotted woodpecker

Guineafowl

Stock dove

Pigeon

TYPES OF FEATHERS

Collecting feathers for decoration was once big business and birds were often killed for their spectacular plumage. Fortunately, this is now banned. Picking up a few feathers isn't illegal and can help you to find out more about different feather types. Stick some onto the following pages, labelling and dating them where possible.

FLIGHT FEATHERS

The large, strong feathers on a bird's wings or tail are called flight feathers. These are light and curved, helping a bird to fly. If you find one, you can carve the end into a nib shape and then dip it in ink to use as a pen.

BODY FEATHERS

These are also called contour feathers. They are smaller and softer towards the end than flight feathers and overlap in a way that enables a bird to maintain body heat. They also help to provide an aerodynamic shape suitable for flying.

DOWN FEATHERS

If you find a small, fluffy feather, it is likely to be a down feather. These lie closest to the skin and help a bird to stay warm. Newly hatched chicks often develop down feathers first, which are then replaced with contour and flight feathers.

DISPLAY FEATHERS

For some birds, showy feathers and elaborate dances are used to attract a mate. Males tend to be the ones with the colourful display feathers which some, like the peacock, use to eye-grabbing effect.

Flight feather

Body feathers

Down feathers

Display feather

Preening
Birds have up to 25,000 feathers that need to be groomed regularly.

43

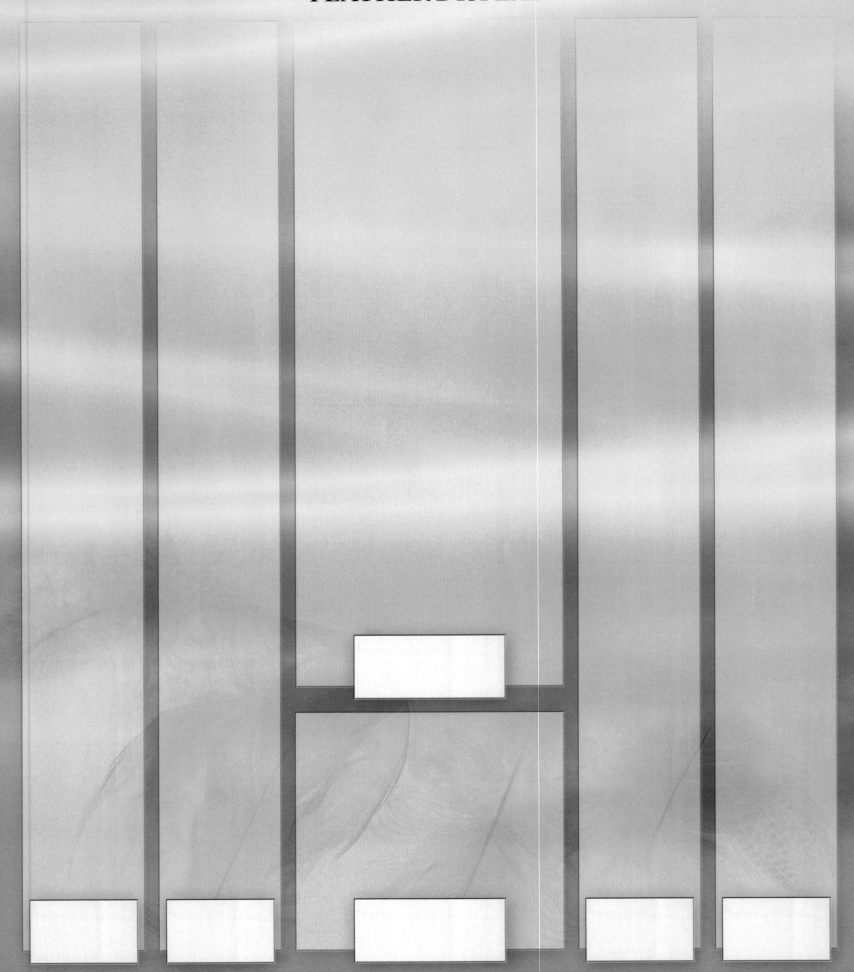

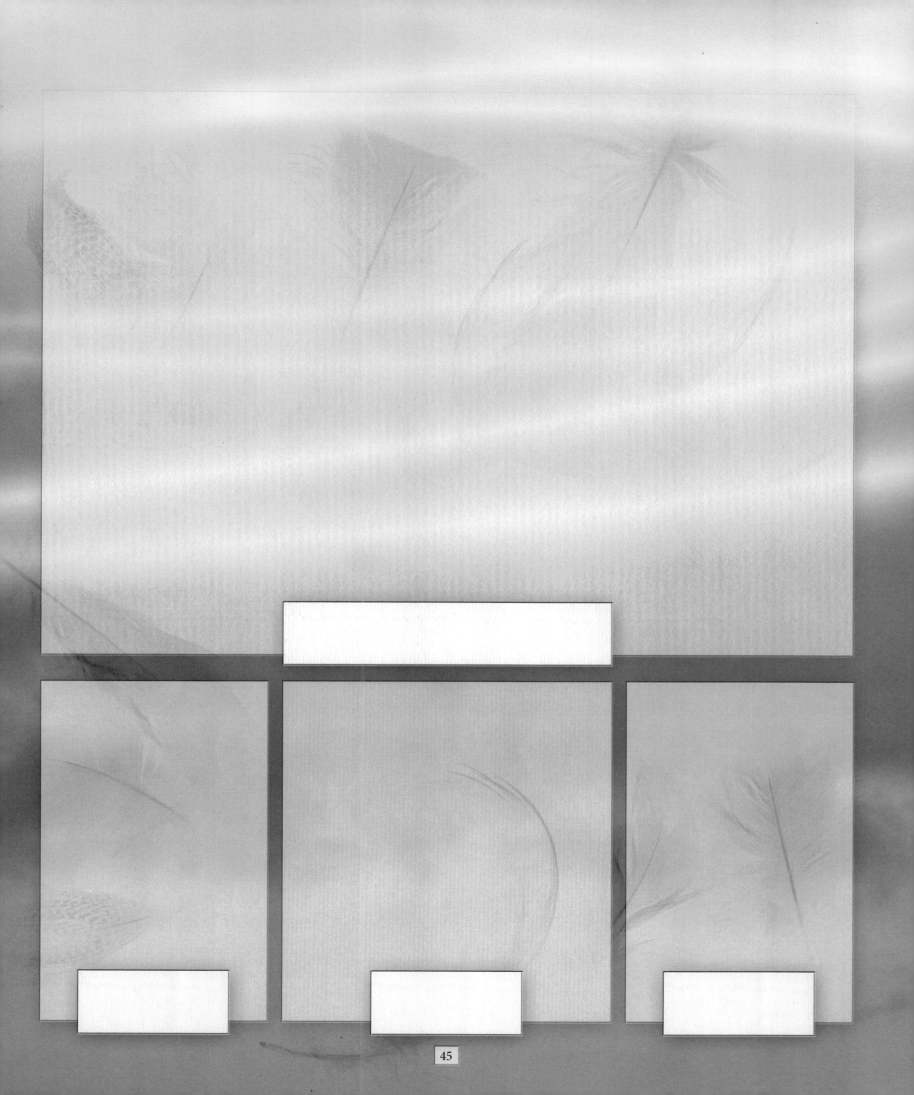

OWL PELLETS

Owls eat small animals whole and get rid of the parts they cannot digest by regurgitating them in the form of pellets. These are usually dry and dusty and they are fascinating to break apart to find out what the owl has been eating. This is likely to be a mixture of bones, feathers, fur, beaks, claws and bits of insects.

WHERE TO FIND THEM

Pellets are grey, dry lumps and their size and shape depend on the species. Look for them around the sites where owls roost, such as at the base of trees and in barns or sheds. Owls produce about two pellets a day, which are usually regurgitated just before they fly off to hunt.

HOW TO DISSECT THEM

Owl pellets don't smell and are quite dry but make sure you wear protective gloves when handling them and wash your hands afterwards. You can soak the pellets first to loosen them up but it isn't essential. Use tweezers or a toothpick to gently tease them apart. Once you have removed the bones, put them into some cleaning solution.

Tawny owl

Pellets
This is what one looks like whole and then taken apart.

HOW TO ORGANISE THEM

Once the bones are clean and dry, sort them into piles according to the type of bones they are. Stick the smaller ones onto the page opposite. For larger items, draw them in the spaces provided here and then store the actual bones elsewhere.

NOTE: Clothes-moth caterpillars often live in pellets, so avoid keeping them indoors.

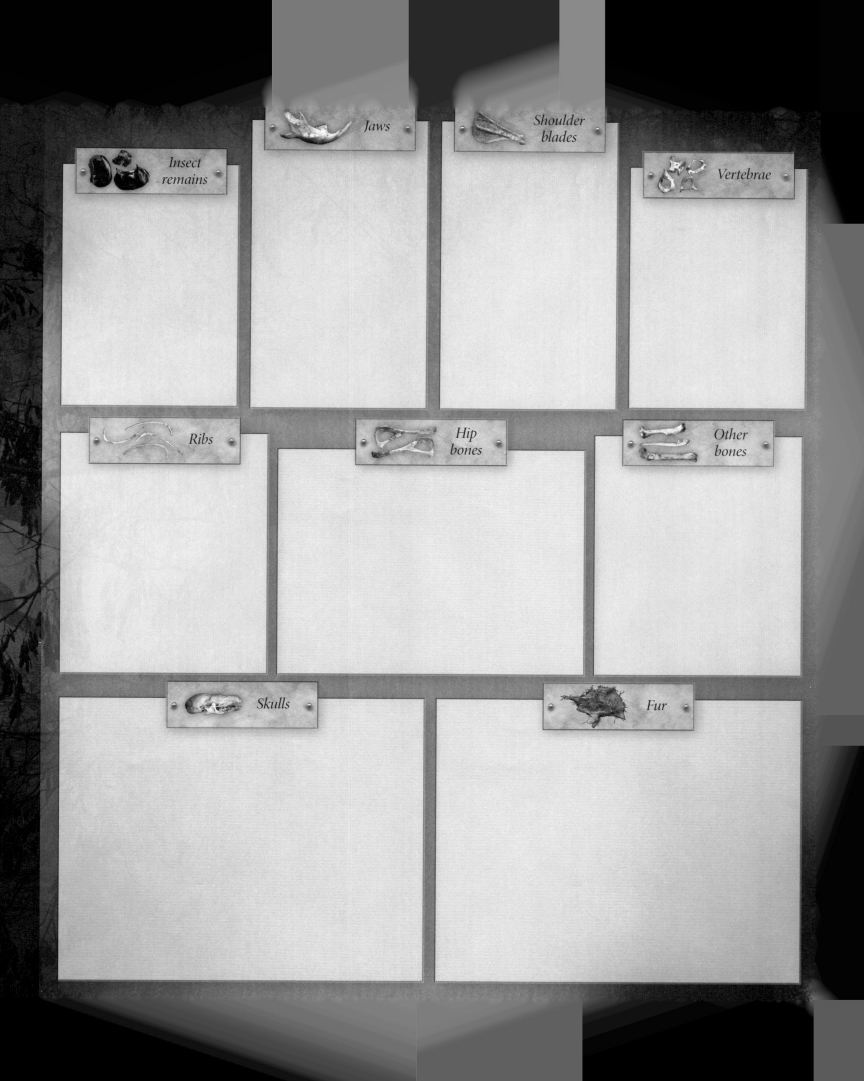

MOTHS

Worldwide, there are at least ten times as many moth as butterfly species. However, moths are harder to see as most fly at night and many are tiny or drab. Moths are attracted to light, so try hanging up a white sheet on a summer's evening and shining a torch onto it and see what arrives. Here are some moths to look out for.

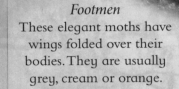

Tiger moths
These bright, day-flying stripy moths have caterpillars that are called woolly bears.

Footmen
These elegant moths have wings folded over their bodies. They are usually grey, cream or orange.

Burnet moths
The red colour warns that these insects are poisonous. Burnets fly by day and have clubbed antennae.

Tussock moths
The adult moths never eat, though the caterpillars do. Look for their furry forelegs and broad wings.

Micro moths
This is the name (short for *microlepidoptera*) given to small moths. Larger ones are called macro moths.

Hawk moths
These large day moths fly quickly. Some hover and they are often mistaken for hummingbirds.

Moth caterpillars
These range from hairy to smooth. Don't touch them as some can cause allergic reactions.

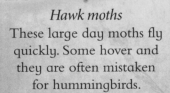

BUTTERFLIES

It used to be common to catch butterflies and moths to form collections. Now it is definitely NOT all right to do this and instead you can create your own photo records. Here are some common butterfly groups and forms and overleaf is a place for you to arrange your own pictures.

Eggs
It helps to research what plants butterflies like to lay their eggs on before you look for them.

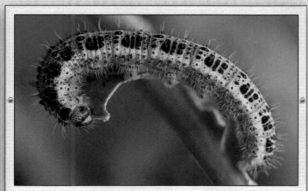

Caterpillars
Leaves covered with chewed holes are a common sign that there are hungry caterpillars feeding nearby.

Chrysalises
These protective cases can be hard to see. Grass verges are a good place to look.

Blues
There are many blue butterfly species and most are small. The sexes are often different colours.

Swallowtails
Easy to spot, these large blousy butterflies can be found throughout the world except for Antarctica.

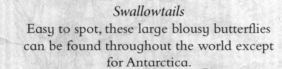

Nymphalids
These are usually medium to large butterflies. Look out for their short front legs.

Skippers
Often looking more like moths, skippers have large hairy bodies, small wings and hooked antennae.

Whites
No prizes for guessing the main colour of these butterflies! They are tricky to photograph as they always seem to be moving.

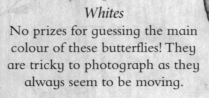

LEPIDOPTERA ALBUM

OTHER INSECTS

Imagine this: about one million insect species have been discovered and there could be about 30 million as yet to find. New species of insect are being reported all the time in every type of habitat, including gardens, parks and even car parks – many by keen nature-watchers. Could the next discovery be yours?

WHERE TO FIND THEM

Insects can be found just about anywhere. Good places to investigate include under stones, bricks and loose bark; through dry leaves and decayed wood; in clumps of weeds and flowers; at the edges of rivers and ponds; and behind doors and windows in your home.

WHAT TO LOOK FOR

Insects fall into different groups according to their appearance and how they behave. Some of the main groups are shown here. See if you can find an insect from each of these categories and put your photos into the empty spaces left next to the images here.

HOW TO EXAMINE THEM

One way to study any insects you come across is to place them gently in glass jars or plastic pots. If you can, photograph them and make a note of where and when you found them. Once you've finished, let the insects go. Photographing and cataloguing insects can be of great help to scientists.

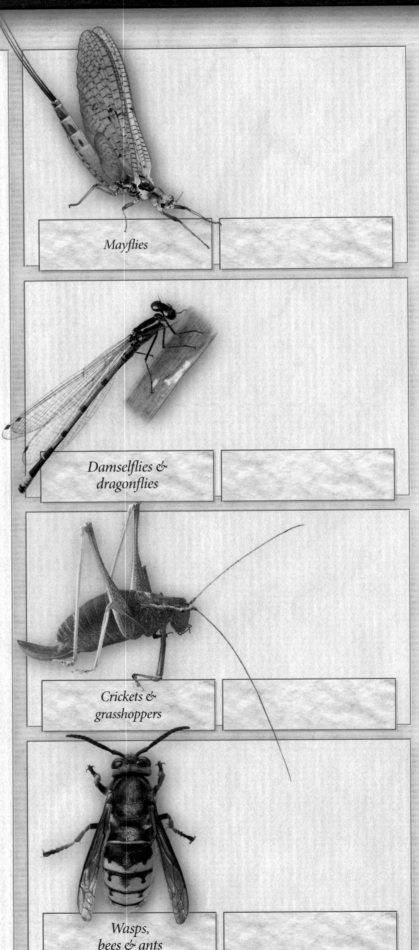

Mayflies

Damselflies & dragonflies

Crickets & grasshoppers

Wasps, bees & ants

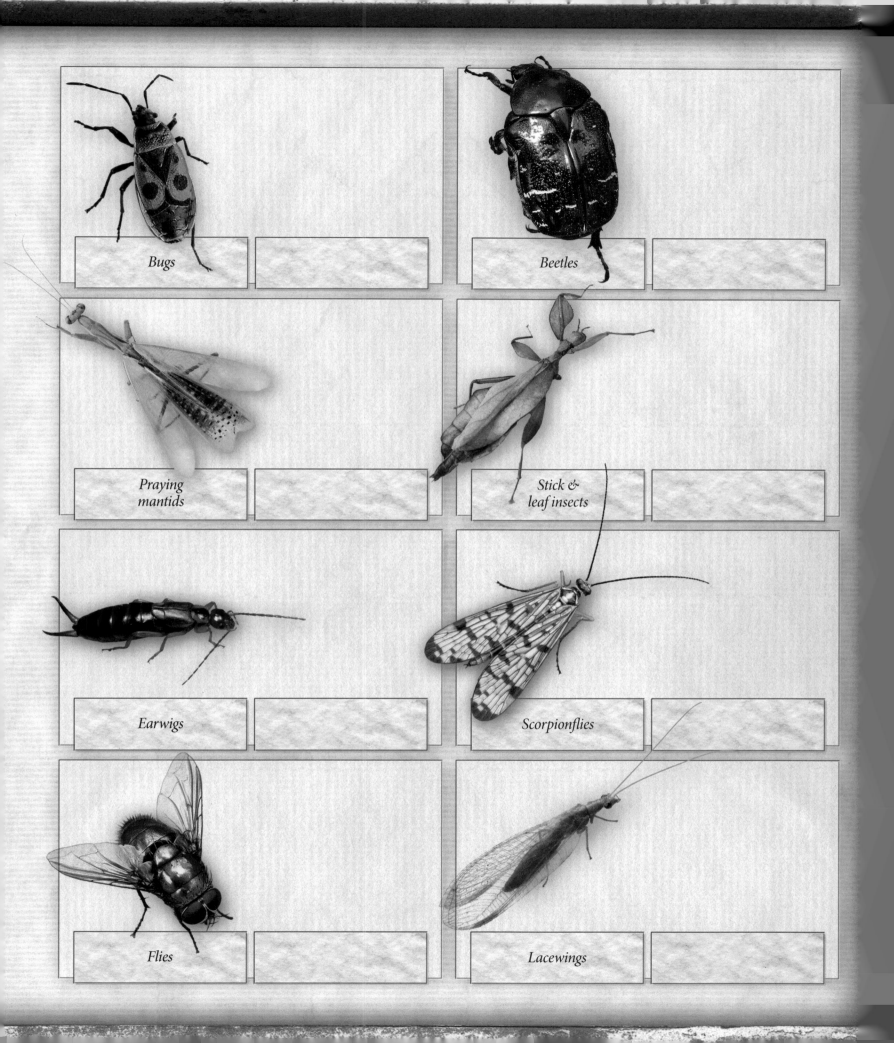

Bugs

Beetles

Praying
mantids

Stick &
leaf insects

Earwigs

Scorpionflies

Flies

Lacewings

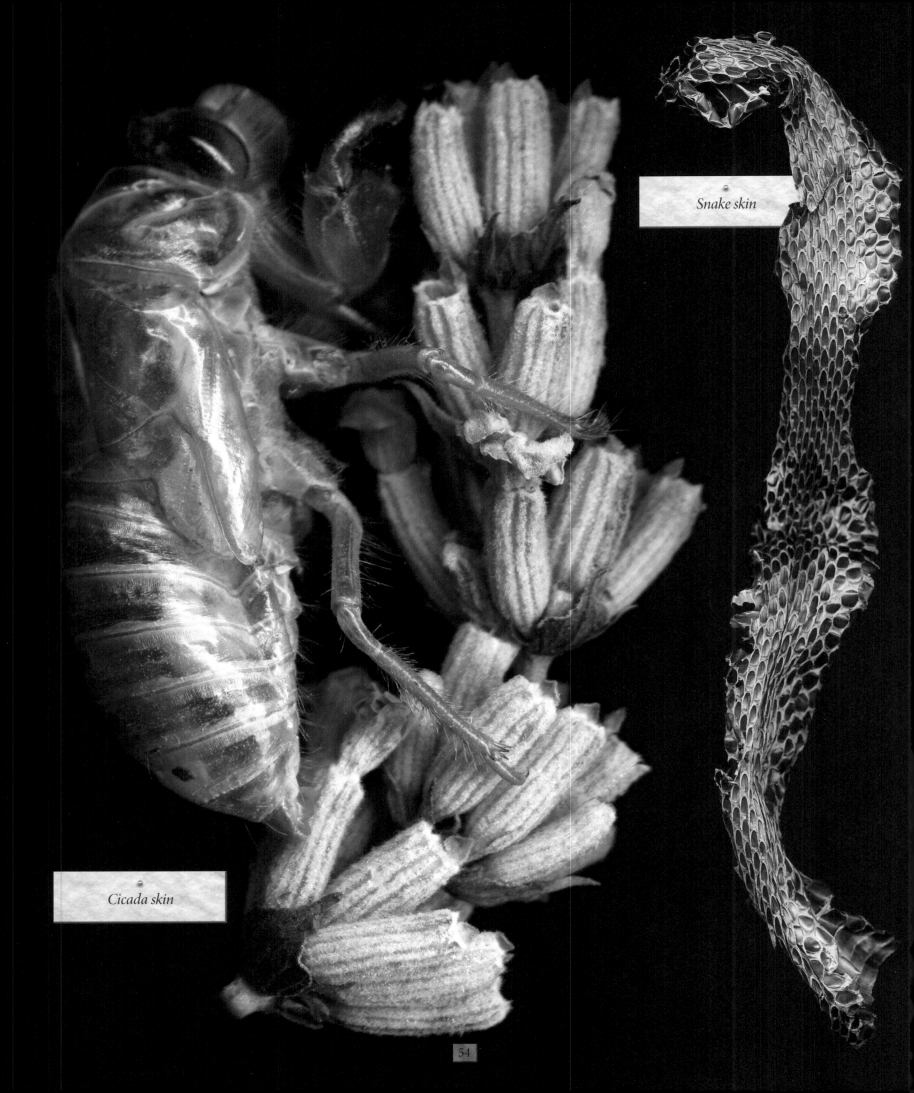

Snake skin

Cicada skin

Grasshopper

chrysalis

Dragonfly nymph case

Damselfly nymph case

EXUVIAE

As intriguing as their name, exuviae are the dried outer casings of animals that are shed as they grow or develop. Animals that go through this process include dragonflies, damselflies, butterflies, moths, cicadas, grasshoppers, mayflies, stoneflies and crickets. The cast-offs are fascinating to collect and provide evidence of how these species are surviving in different habitats.

COLLECTING EXUVIAE

These ghostly remains often mark the end of a stage of an insect's development as it finally emerges into adult form. They are reasonably easy to find if you know what to look for. Insects are not the only ones to shed their outer casings – keep an eye out for other cast-offs such as snake skins and crab shells.

WHERE TO LOOK

The best place to discover dragonfly and damselfly exuviae is on the reeds around ponds and rivers in late spring and summer. The nymphs crawl up, their backs split open and the adults emerge and fly off. Cicada exuviae are found on trees, and empty butterfly and moth chrysalis cases can be found almost anywhere.

GATHERING AND STORING THEM

Slide empty dragonfly and damselfly cases along the plant stems to ease them off. The legs are very fragile and may break, but splashing some water on the case makes it more flexible. As with all specimens, it is essential to make sure they are completely dry before you store them, to prevent them from decaying.

LABELLING SAMPLES

It is always a good idea to label each specimen with details of what it is and where and when you found it. It is possible to identify the species and sex of the insect from the exuviae, though this involves a reasonable amount of research and patience.

SPORES

If you turn a fungus upside-down, look to see
if it has ridge-like gills under the cap. If it does,
these contain spores. Spores are tiny particles
released by some fungi as a way to reproduce.
If the conditions are right, the spores develop
into sporelings, thereby forming new fungi.

SPORE PRINTS

The spores themselves are invisible to the naked eye
but lots of them together can be seen like specks of
dust. Not all gills and spores are the same colour, so
you can make something called a spore print to help
you identify different specimens.

Gills on the underside of a fungus cap

PREPARING THE FUNGI

A mature fungus with a flat, open cap makes the best
spore print. A supermarket mushroom is a good place
to start. If you use a wild one, make sure you know
what it is, as some fungi are extremely poisonous.

RELEASING THE SPORES

Cut off the stalk and put the fungus gill-side down
onto a piece of card. Place a bowl over the top of it
and leave it overnight. Carefully remove the bowl and
cap the next morning and see what pattern has been
made by the spores. Use a fixative, such as hairspray,
to prevent the spore print from blowing away.

SPORE STORE

FROM DAWN TO DUSK

Sunlight changes from day to day and all day long as well. It takes 8.3 minutes for light to reach us from the Sun, and how it appears to us depends on many factors including where you live in the world, the season, the time of day and how much cloud cover is overhead.

SUNRISE AND SUNSET

Light is made up of different colours and when the sun is low in the sky, it has to travel further through the atmosphere. This scatters the bluer, colder colours leaving the warmer red ones. As the day moves into twilight, the light changes and becomes much bluer as the red colours now pass straight into space.

LIGHT THROUGH THE SEASONS

There are fewer hours of daylight in the winter but, strangely, it can often seem lighter as many trees lack leaves and grasses have died back. In contrast, the sharp greens of spring and the dark greens of summer provide a wealth of shady places until die-back in autumn makes the world seem lighter again.

Sunset after a storm

COLLECTING LIGHT

To illustrate how the light changes during the course of one day, try the simple experiment shown in the boxes here. Take a photo from the same spot at hourly intervals, then print them out and stick the ones that show the greatest light change onto the page opposite. You could also try taking different scenes, or a sequence of sunrise and sunset shots instead.

6 am

8 am

9 am

10 am

3 pm

6 pm

7 pm

9 pm

LIGHT GALLERY

You only notice things if you stay in one place for a time. DAVID HOCKNEY, artist (born 1937)

WATER

YOU NEVER MISS THE WATER
TILL THE WELL RUNS DRY.

PROVERB

Puddles, ponds, lakes, rivers, seas and oceans – water covers almost three-quarters of the Earth's surface. Only a tiny fraction of this is the fresh water that we depend upon for our survival. Dive into the following pages to discover ways to make the most out of the time you spend in different watery habitats. Stay safe, have fun and, as the proverb implies, cherish every drop.

Predicting rain

Watery weather

Pond dipping

Beachcombing

Seashells

Tadpoles

Seaweeds

MY WATER COLLECTION

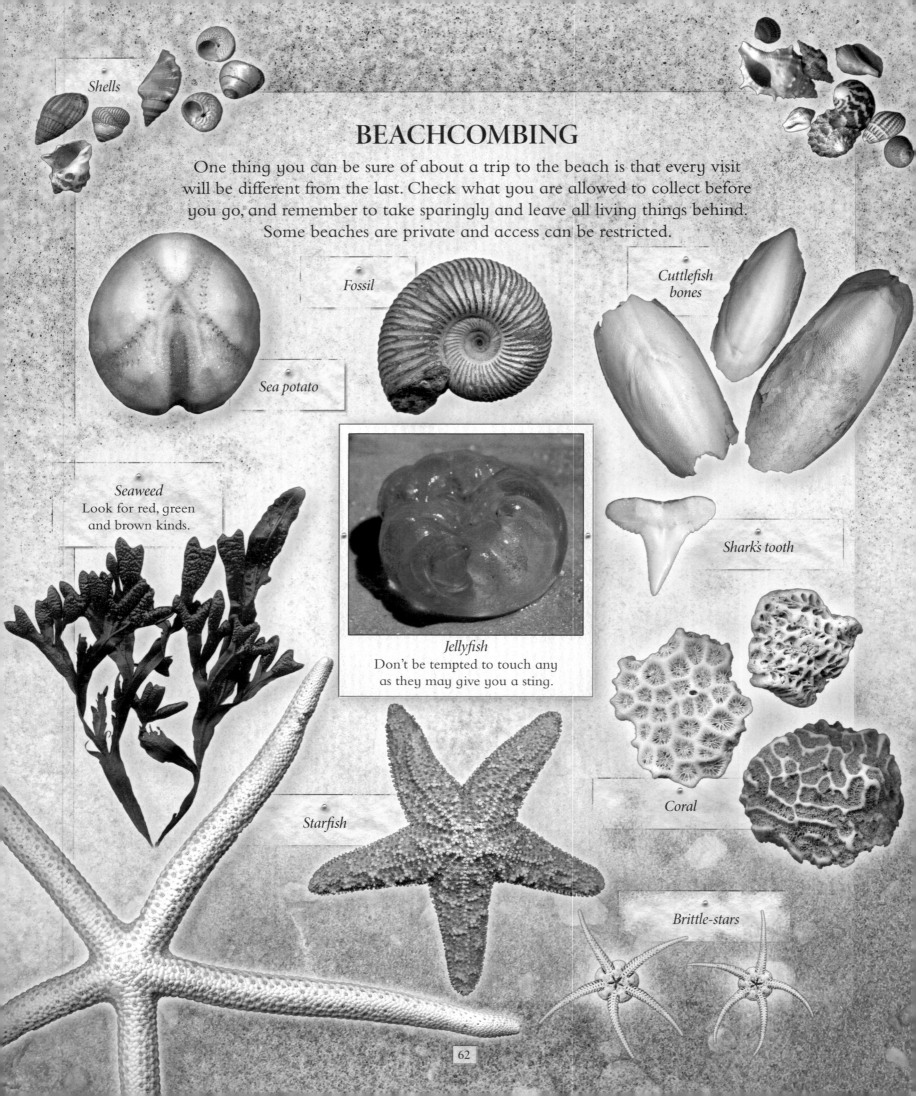

BEACHCOMBING

One thing you can be sure of about a trip to the beach is that every visit will be different from the last. Check what you are allowed to collect before you go, and remember to take sparingly and leave all living things behind. Some beaches are private and access can be restricted.

Shells

Fossil

Sea potato

Cuttlefish bones

Seaweed
Look for red, green and brown kinds.

Jellyfish
Don't be tempted to touch any as they may give you a sting.

Shark's tooth

Starfish

Coral

Brittle-stars

Whelk egg case

A GUIDE TO BEACHCOMBING

The best time to go beachcombing is at low tide, especially after a storm when objects tend to get thrown up onto the beach. Whatever type of beach you go to, there will always be zones where different animals and plants live. Frequent visits will help you become familiar with these zones and what you can expect to find in them.

Sea urchin tests

WHERE TO LOOK

Start by scanning the tide lines on a beach. These are where most debris is left. There may be as many as three separate tide lines. The lowest one marks the normal high-tide line; the next, which is usually a bit higher up, is from the last spring or full-moon tide; and the highest line will have been formed by the most recent storm.

WHAT TO COLLECT

Remember to take along some collecting bags or a bucket. If you aren't sure whether something is alive or not, leave it. Many of the objects you collect can be used to make pictures, while other things can be kept on display at home. Remember to clean items in your collection thoroughly before storing them or they will soon start to smell.

Mermaid's purses

WHAT TO LEAVE

Don't take jellyfish, starfish, sand dollars, living shellfish, bits of coral or stranded animals. You can always take pictures of things that are interesting but can't be taken away, or make a sketch of them instead. Remember to make a note of when, where and what you find.

Driftwood
Try carving it into interesting shapes.

Animal remains
Make sure you give them a good clean.

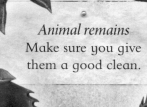

Sand dollar test

SEAWEEDS

Seaweeds are simple non-flowering algae. There are three kinds – red, brown and green – and you are most likely to find them on rocky shores. Make sure you have permission to collect the seaweeds where you are and that they are not in an area of special scientific interest.

Irish moss

Fucus

COLLECTING SEAWEEDS

You can press seaweeds in the same way as flowers, although it can be a little tricky. Fine ones make better pictures, and a mixture of colours also works well. Collect them in a container with enough seawater to keep the seaweeds damp.

Knotted wrack

Dulse

MAKING PICTURES

Put a piece of watercolour paper in a plastic tray and pour in enough seawater to just cover it. Take individual pieces of seaweeds and arrange them on the paper to form pictures. It is a good idea to trim the thicker bits, otherwise they will stick together and the branching patterns will be less clear.

PRESSING THEM

Gently lift your picture out of the bowl, keeping it flat, then carefully tip off any excess water. The weed has a natural glue, so find some sort of mesh to put directly on top of it. Next, place a sheet of blotting paper over the mesh and put the whole lot in a flower press or under some heavy weight. Leave it for at least two weeks, then carefully remove your picture from the press.

Japweed

Sea lettuce

Serrated wrack

Irish moss

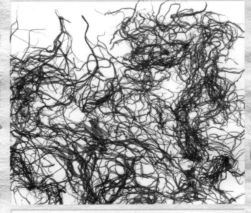

Gut weed

Bladderwrack

Kelp

SEASHELLS

Shells are home to soft-bodied animals called molluscs. They create the shells as they grow, forming a protective case around themselves. There are many different ways of organising shell collections, such as by colour, size or location. Here is a simple guide to arranging them by shape.

Murex

Club shape

Lightning whelk

Ear shape

Abalone

Pear shape

Whelk

Frog shells

Cap shape

SINGLE SHELLS

Molluscs with one shell are called gastropods and their shells are often coiled. Look down the shell tip to see which way it coils – most run clockwise.

Corkscrew shape

Tower shells

Limpets

Top shape

Top shells

Barrel shape

False fusus

Cowries

Spindle shape

Tun

Egg shape

Turrid

Scotch bonnet

66

Discus shape

Paddle shape

Mussels

Clams

Triangular shape

Tellins

DOUBLE SHELLS

Look for these molluscs, which are also known as
bivalves, on sandy shores. They have shells made up
of two halves, though often you will find only one.

Razor shell

Fan shape

Boat shape

Scallops

Cockles

Ark shell

Piddock

HOW TO COLLECT SHELLS

The most vital thing to remember is to gather only abandoned shells and
limit the number you take. When you get home, wash them in warm, soapy
water using a toothbrush, then rinse and dry them. Have fun creating
collections in old boxes or drawers and on shelves. If you can, label each one
giving the name, location and the date it was found.

TADPOLES

There are only a few animals that you can keep as temporary pets and tadpoles are one of them. It can be fun to watch them grow into adults – but don't expect too much give on the emotional front.

GATHERING SPAWN

Start looking from early spring for clumps of frogspawn in ponds and rivers. Collect only a few eggs in a jar or bucket, and make sure you take enough water to fill the container you intend to keep them in.

CARING FOR TADPOLES

Ensure that you put them in a cool place and keep the container topped up with pond water. Feed them bits of pond weed or goldfish food daily and watch them grow. Add rocks for the young frogs to sit on.

RETURNING THEM TO THE WILD

It takes up to 16 weeks for frogs to turn into adults. When you release them, make sure you go back to the same pond they came from. Draw or stick pictures of your growing tadpoles on the page opposite.

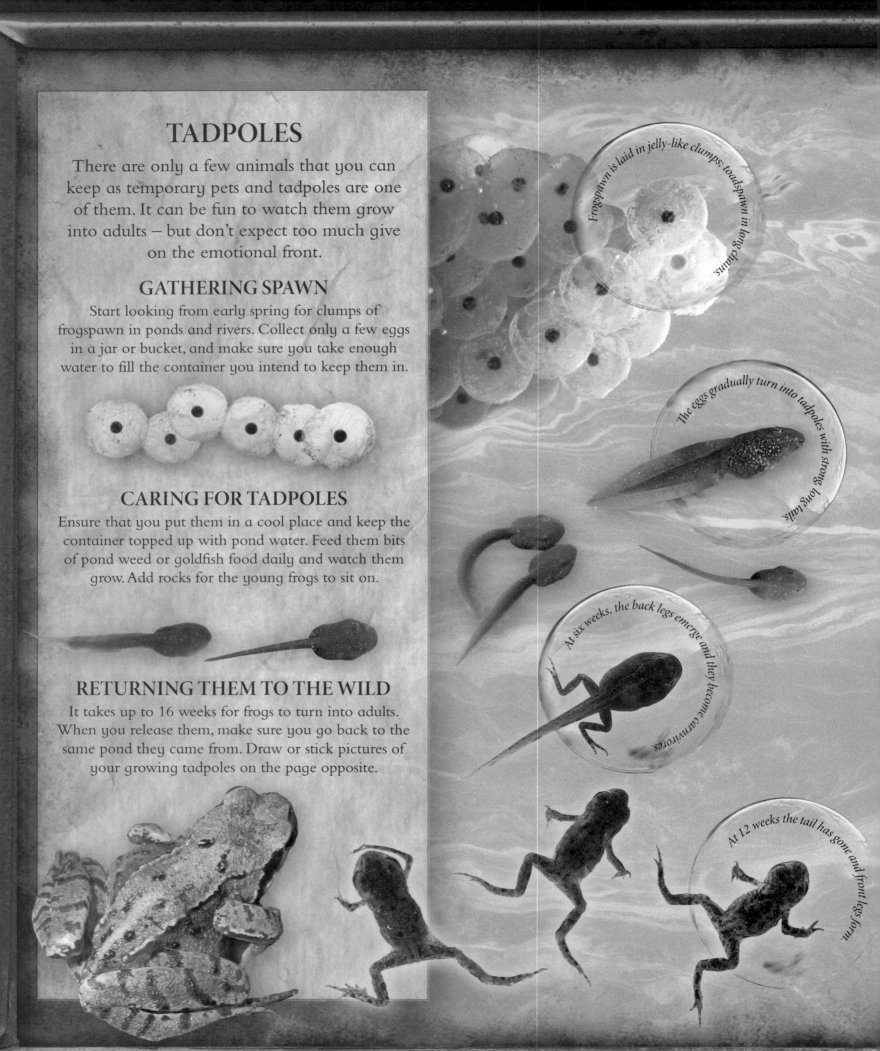

Frogspawn is laid in jelly-like clumps; toadspawn in long chains.

The eggs gradually turn into tadpoles with strong, long tails.

At six weeks, the back legs emerge and they become carnivores.

At 12 weeks the tail has gone and front legs form.

A TANK FOR TADPOLES

Mayflies

Dragonflies

Damselflies

Newts

Pond snails

Water boatmen

Toadspawn

Water beetles

Pond skaters

Damselfly nymphs

Pea clams

Pond weed

Sticklebacks

POND DIPPING

Hours of fun can be had with a net and a bucket or tray by the side of ponds and rivers. Each time you dip your net in, you are sure to find something different, and some of the creatures that turn up may look as if they are from another planet.

WHAT YOU WILL NEED

Take a net with a fine mesh weave and, ideally, a shallow plastic tray. However, a jam jar or any clean container would work just as well. A magnifying glass is useful for examining specimens, as are a pen and a notebook to record your finds.

HOW TO POND DIP

Animals like to hide around plants in the shallows, so try looking here first. Sweep your net through the water, then tip out the contents into a container. Once you have had a good look, note what is there, then carefully pour the water back into the pond.

WHAT YOU MAY FIND

In addition to the creatures shown here, you may also come across the larvae of water beetles, dragonflies and damselflies, which are as aggressive as they look. You may also catch sight of small fish such as minnows, large freshwater mussels, shrimps, crayfish and maybe the odd grass snake. Make a picture collection of your discoveries in the spaces left here.

PREDICTING RAIN

Black clouds outside? Wind's up? More than likely it is going to rain. Until it is almost upon you, it can be tricky trying to predict it. However, there are a number of signs that rain is on its way – some more reliable than others.

When clouds appear like rocks and towers, Earth's refreshed by frequent showers. PROVERB

EYES TO THE SKIES

Clouds are made up of water droplets or ice crystals, so if there are more clouds, there is a greater chance that it will rain. Nimbus clouds produce rain, hail, sleet or snow, while other clouds can also mean that rain is on the way.

Cirrus clouds or mare's tails
Unlike most high clouds, these often mean rain is approaching.

Nimbostratus clouds
If you are outside and you see these, get inside! If it is not raining already, it soon will be.

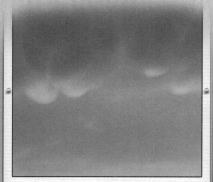

Mammatus clouds
These strange sinking clouds signal thunderstorms nearby.

LOOKING FOR OTHER SKY SIGNS

Many striking effects in the sky are caused by the sun bouncing off ice crystals in clouds to create vivid colours. Below are two examples. A ring around the sun or moon is another similar phenomenon to watch out for.

Red sky in the morning
... sailors take warning. Like many old sayings, this has some truth in it, so do look out for rain.

Sun dogs
These often occur when the sun is low in the sky. There may be one on each side of the sun.

FEELING THE AIR

Strong winds often mean that bad weather is approaching. Look to see which way the wind is coming from and how forceful it is. When rain is due, some people can feel a change in the air, in the same way that it is possible to sense the changing seasons.

Wind direction
Look to see which way the trees are blowing to find out where the wind is coming from.

Rich smells
Before rain, the ground releases stronger smells. Once the rain has passed, plants smell more, too.

WATCHING ANIMAL & PLANT BEHAVIOUR

Changes in animal behaviour are not a fail-safe way of knowing whether a deluge is due. However, animals can smell, hear and see things that we cannot, so who knows for sure? Plants are possibly more reliable indicators of rain being imminent, but a note of caution is still necessary.

Bees staying close to home
Most insects fly less when it is raining or temperatures drop.

Cows lying down
Perhaps the best-known – but generally not the most accurate – way of forecasting rain.

Mistle thrushes singing
Also called stormcocks, these birds sing when storms near.

Flowers closing
The flowers of the scarlet pimpernel close up before it starts to rain.

Dew on the grass
If there is dew on the grass, then it is said to be unlikely to rain that day.

Cones closing
These close before rain to prevent the seeds from escaping.

Rainbow

Fog

Rain

Mist

Hail

Snow

Frost

WATERY WEATHER

Just watching rain or snow fall outside is entertaining. However, you can discover more by making a simple measuring gauge. Take a plastic bottle and cut off the top third. Place it upside-down into the bottom part of the bottle and put it somewhere outside where it won't blow over. Mark a scale on the side and use it to measure how much rain or snow falls in your area. Write down your findings opposite and add some pictures to create your own weather board.

Ice

WEATHER BOARD

ALL THROUGH THE YEAR

A place for you to stick in favourite things from each month of the year.

FIELD NOTES

A space for you to write down any nature thoughts.

WHERE NEXT AS A NATURALIST?

By the time you reach this page, this book should feel alive with all the things you have put inside it and be a very personal record of all the times you have spent outside. If you would like to continue exploring nature, but are not sure how or where to go about it, here are some ideas.

CARRY ON COLLECTING

We cannot stress enough the fact that many things need to be left where you find them, but you can use the things you are allowed to gather to form some amazing nature displays. From nothing, you can soon amass a really interesting collection that friends and relations will no doubt find fascinating. Once you are known to have an interest in nature, you may discover that people bring you the oddest things as gifts.

Part of the Fine Feather Press collection

VISIT US ONLINE

Go to www.finefeatherpress.com to find links to downloadable templates to help you with the activities in this book, such as decorated seed packets, further printable collecting pages and labels for bottles and jars.

If you would like suggestions on how to organise your own scrapbook pages or nature displays at home, we've also posted some of our Fine Feather Press ones for you to browse through.

JOIN AN ORGANISATION

If you have enjoyed this book and want to take a more active part in helping to look after the natural world, there are many nature societies that you can join. Here are some of them.

Action for Conservation
Amateur Entomological Society
Association of British Fungus Groups
Bat Conservation Trust
Bees, Wasps and Ants Recording Society
British Dragonfly Society
British Herpetological Society (Reptiles & Amphibians)
British Trust for Ornithology (Birds)
Buglife – The Invertebrate Conservation Trust
Bumblebee Conservation Trust
Butterfly Conservation
Forestry Commission
Forest Schools Association
Froglife
John Muir Trust (Protecting Wild Land)
Mammal Society
Marine Conservation Society
Natural History Museum
National Trust
People's Trust for Endangered Species
Plantlife
Project Wild Thing
Royal Society for the Protection of Birds
Scottish Wildlife Trust
The Conservation Volunteers
Whale and Dolphin Conservation Society
Wildfowl and Wetlands Trust
Wildlife Trusts
Woodland Trust
World Wildlife Fund for Nature

Please note that the organisations listed here have not necessarily endorsed this book.

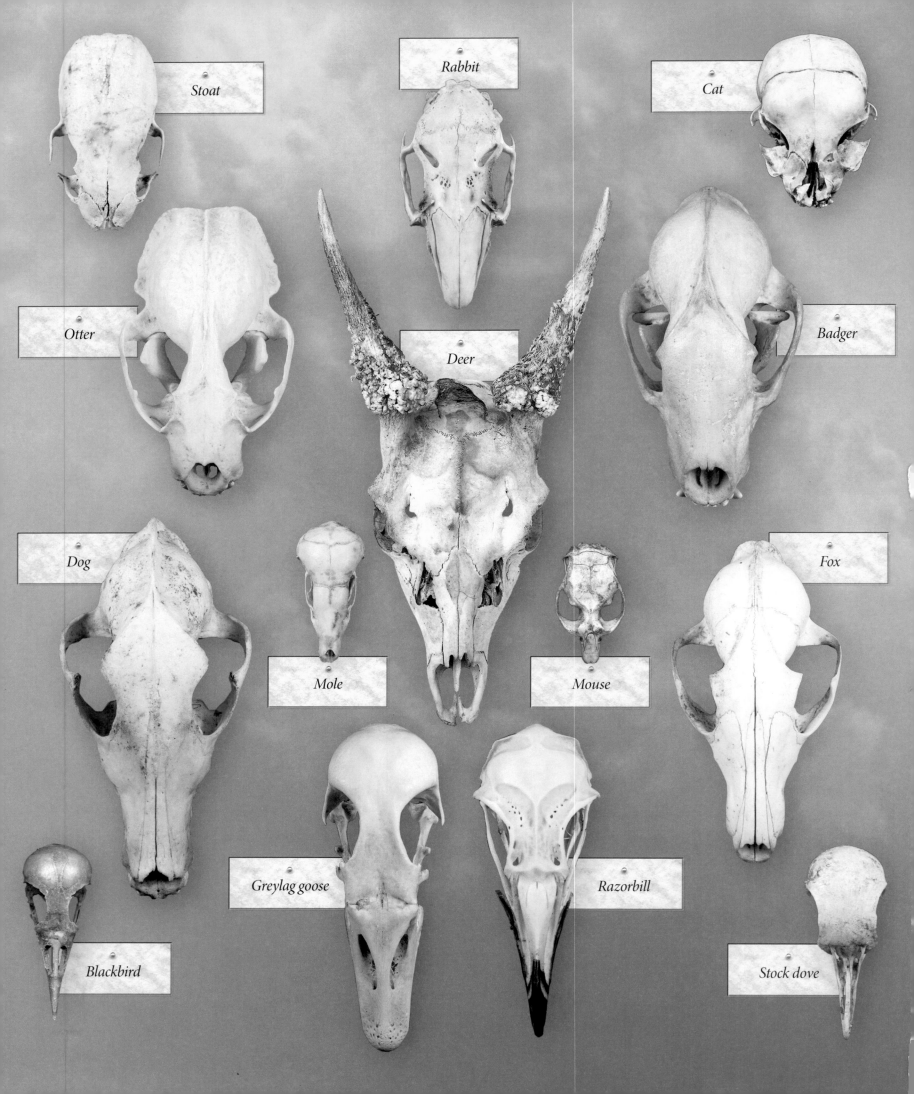

Stoat

Rabbit

Cat

Otter

Deer

Badger

Dog

Mole

Mouse

Fox

Blackbird

Greylag goose

Razorbill

Stock dove